Witty
Comebacks

Witty
Comebacks

Great responses and
sassy remarks

SIRIUS

SIRIUS

This edition published in 2020 by Sirius Publishing, a division of
Arcturus Publishing Limited,
26/27 Bickels Yard, 151–153 Bermondsey Street,
London SE1 3HA

ISBN: 978-1-83857-613-4
AD007316UK

Printed in Singapore

Contents

Introduction.................................. 6

1. Returned with interest.............. 9
2. Political brickbats 33
3. Disrespectfully yours................ 71
4. Work in progress..................... 93
5. Slings and arrows 107
6. Heckles 139
7. Cut....................................... 155
8. Cruel to be kind..................... 179
9. Modesty permits..................... 203
10. Mob rule OK 217
11. On the spot.......................... 239
12. Naughty but nice 279
13. The last laugh 301

Introduction

We've all been there. Somebody gives you offence and you come away fuming. Then, gradually, you begin to think of all the witty things you should have said to cut them to the quick and win the day. You need practice and this book is here to help.

Even Oscar Wilde, one of the masters of the witty one-liner, experienced that 'I wish I'd said that' feeling. But not often. He practised the art of eloquence at every possible moment – even on his way to prison – and consequently his clever comebacks are well documented. But here they are joined by a plethora of pithy ripostes from other protagonists, including some from – wait for it – ordinary people!

That's right. From the corridors of Westminster to the Hollywood Hills to the post-it note on the office fridge, you'll find clever comebacks that will make you smile. And that's the golden rule: there has to be wit.

Mere name-calling doesn't cut it. As Dorothy Parker (who also features prominently in these pages) once said, 'Wit has truth in it. Wisecracking is simply calisthenics with words.'

This book is a testament to the human ability to rescue victory from the jaws of defeat with one undeniable flourish of the laconic lance.

But not all the comebacks in this collection are the final shot in a war of words. Some are self-effacing, some saucy, some assertive, some surreal. The beauty of the witty comeback is that it comes in all sorts of styles and can reflect the full spectrum of human sentiments.

I hope you find plenty here to inspire you to victory in your next game of verbal tennis. And if you don't, please keep it to yourself.

Tim Glynne-Jones, compiler

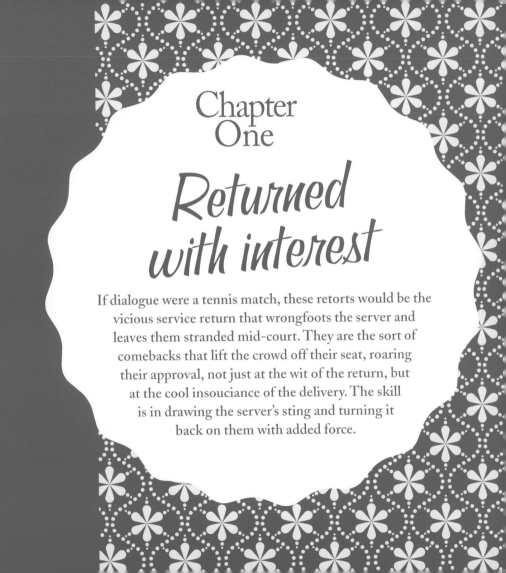

Chapter One

Returned with interest

If dialogue were a tennis match, these retorts would be the vicious service return that wrongfoots the server and leaves them stranded mid-court. They are the sort of comebacks that lift the crowd off their seat, roaring their approval, not just at the wit of the return, but at the cool insouciance of the delivery. The skill is in drawing the server's sting and turning it back on them with added force.

Returned with interest

Let's begin with two of the most famous winning
returns of all. Both are credited to Winston Churchill,
although the first one is much more likely to have been
uttered (though not originated) by his friend F. E.
Smith. It occurred in an exchange with Lady Astor at a
party at Blenheim Palace and it goes like this:

'If I were your wife, I would put poison in your tea.'

'If I were your husband, I would drink it.'

But this immortal exchange with the redoubtable Labour politician Bessie Braddock was Churchill's.

'Winston, you are drunk!'

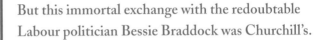

'Bessie, my dear, you are ugly. But I shall be sober in the morning.'

Returned with interest

Muhammad Ali once refused to fasten his seatbelt on a plane, saying:

'Superman don't need no seatbelt.'

Unfazed, the stewardess delighted the whole plane by pointing out:

'Superman don't need no airplane neither.'

Former Governor of New York, Al Smith, was once stopped mid-speech by a heckler, who shouted:

'Go ahead, Al, don't let me bother you. Tell 'em all you know. It won't take long.'

Smith quickly silenced the man with the retort:

'If I tell 'em all we both know, it won't take me any longer.'

Returned with interest

A classic comeback is recorded from the Greek statesman Alcibiades against his uncle, Pericles.

The latter said patronisingly:

'When I was your age, Alcibiades, I talked just the way you are now talking.'

The nephew came back with:

'If only I had known you, Pericles, when you were at your best.'

Returned with interest

Author Clare Booth Luce once stepped aside to let fellow writer Dorothy Parker through a door with the following invitation:

'Age before beauty.'

Parker coolly accepted the gesture, replying:

'Pearls before swine.'

Returned with interest

'Sledging' (verbally intimidating the opposition) is an aspect of cricket that sometimes spills over into nastiness. On these occasions, a cool head usually wins the day. England cricket captain Mike Atherton, while playing a Test match in Australia, dismissed the sledging of Australia's Ian Healy, who called him a cheat, with the wonderfully English response:

"When in Rome, dear boy."

On another occasion, the Australian bowlers were getting frustrated at not being able to get the Sri Lankan batsman Arjuna Ranatunga out. He was rather overweight at the time.

The Australians tried everything they knew to bamboozle him, but he remained at the crease hitting the bowling to every corner of the ground.

That was when Ian Healy, the wicketkeeper, spoke up:

'Put a Mars bar on a good length and that should do it.'

In a similar vein, one of the most legendary ripostes was uttered by 18th-century British radical John Wilkes, in response to a dig from his adversary Lord Montagu. Montagu launched at Wilkes with the insult:

'Pray, Wilkes, I don't know whether you will die on the gallows or of the pox?'

Wilkes replied:

'Why, that will depend, my lord, on whether I embrace your principles or your mistress.'

American writer Edna Ferber was one person who had the measure of flamboyant wit Noel Coward and put him firmly back in his box with this exchange.

Coward: 'Edna, you look almost like a man.'

Ferber:

'So do you.'

Returned with interest

Writers George Bernard Shaw and G. K. Chesterton sometimes exchanged unpleasantries, usually on the subject of their contrasting physical build. Chesterton was portly, Shaw was thin. On one occasion, Chesterton is alleged to have said to his adversary:

'Looking at you, Shaw, one would think there was a famine in the land.'

In response to which, Shaw looked Chesterton over and said:

' Looking at you, one would think you caused it.'

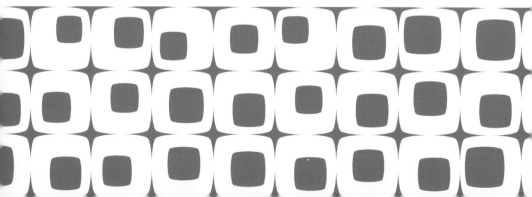

Comedian and composer Oscar Levant once provoked
George Gershwin, saying:

'George, if you had to do it all over, would you still fall in love
with yourself?'

Gershwin coolly replied:

'Oscar, why don't you play us a medley of your hit?'

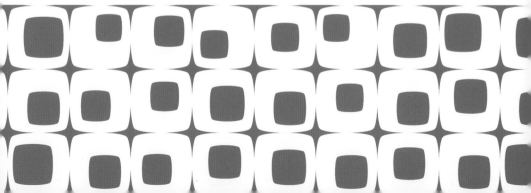

Returned with interest

British boxer Henry Cooper was a gentleman outside the ring but on one occasion he is reported as hitting back at boxing abolitionist Baroness Edith Summerskill with a fearsome counterpunch that echoed Churchill's 'I'll be sober in the morning.'

'Mr Cooper,' she said, 'have you looked in the mirror lately and seen the state of your nose?'

Cooper administered his knockout blow:

'Well, madam, have you looked in the mirror and seen the state of your nose? Boxing is my excuse. What's yours?'

Hermann Adler, chief rabbi of London, was at a dinner where Herbert Vaughan, cardinal of Westminster, was also present. Vaughan asked mischievously when he would be able to share 'this most excellent ham' with Adler.

Quick as a flash, the rabbi offered:

'How about at your eminence's wedding?'

Returned with interest

The actress and writer Ilka Chase was approached by a rival, who offered the barbed:

'I thought your book was wonderful. I can't tell you how much I enjoyed it. By the way, who wrote it for you?'

Chase replied:

'Darling, I'm so glad you liked it. By the way, who read it to you?'

Actress Sandra Bernhardt was once told by an imperious theatre co-owner:

'If I were alone in this, I wouldn't give you a contract.'

Her response:

'If you were alone in this, monsieur, I wouldn't sign.'

Jewish writer Israel Zangwill was chastised at a dinner for yawning.

'Mind your Jewish manners!' said the lady opposite him. 'I thought you were going to swallow me.'

Zangwill replied:

'Have no fear, madam, my religion prohibits my doing that.'

American comedian Jack E. Leonard is famous for this put-down:

'There is nothing wrong with you that reincarnation won't cure.'

Returned with interest

Mark Twain was once challenged by a Mormon to 'cite a single passage of scripture which forbids polygamy'.

Twain was ready:

'Certainly. "No man can serve two masters."'

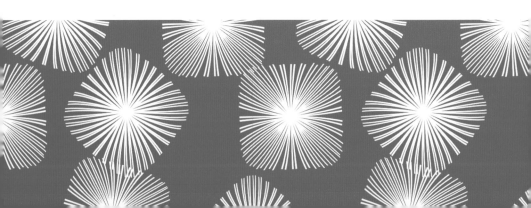

Richard Busby was the headmaster of Westminster School in London and a man of short stature. One time a much larger man squeezed past him in a restaurant, saying sarcastically:

'May I pass to my seat, oh giant?'

Busby replied: 'Certainly, oh pygmy.'

The large man suddenly realized who he was addressing and replied apologetically: 'My expression alluded to the size of your intellect.'

Busby, unrelenting, said:

'And my expression to the size of yours.'

Returned with interest

With some comebacks, you wonder how they came to be recorded and by whom. It could only be the perpetrator relating the incident at a later date. That shouldn't, however, diminish their appeal. For example, while out walking, the playwright Richard Brinsley Sheridan found himself sandwiched by two lords, who told him they had just been debating whether he was a rogue or a fool. Looking from one to the other, Sheridan said:

'Why, I do believe I am between both.'

English writer and clergyman Sydney Smith was a renowned exponent of that 18th-century style of wit that could cut a man to the quick with a well-formed retort. Witness this exchange with a local squire.

Squire: 'If I had a son who was an idiot, by Jove, I'd make him a parson.'

Rev. Sydney Smith:

'Very probably, but I see your father was of a different mind.'

Returned with interest

Napoleon's Foreign Minister Charles Maurice de Talleyrand once found himself being browbeaten by an overbearing general, who kept using the word 'weaklings'. When Talleyrand asked him who he meant by this term, the general said, 'We call weakling anybody who is not military.'

Talleyrand nodded his understanding and replied:

'Ah, as we call military all those who are not civil.'

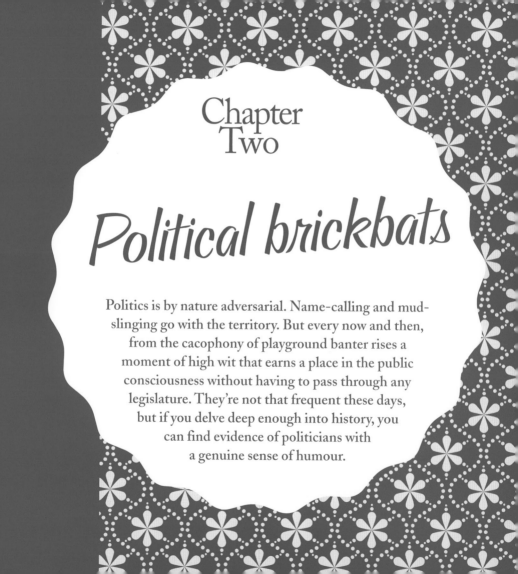

Chapter Two

Political brickbats

Politics is by nature adversarial. Name-calling and mud-slinging go with the territory. But every now and then, from the cacophony of playground banter rises a moment of high wit that earns a place in the public consciousness without having to pass through any legislature. They're not that frequent these days, but if you delve deep enough into history, you can find evidence of politicians with a genuine sense of humour.

Political brickbats

When Adlai Stevenson was running for president, a supporter said to him:

'Governor, every thinking person will be voting for you.'

Stevenson replied:

'Madam, that's not enough. I need a majority.'

William Gladstone and Benjamin Disraeli were arch-rivals in British politics and Disraeli took great delight in belittling his opponent with witty retorts. Here are a few of them.

When asked to pass comment on the character of Gladstone, Disraeli quipped:

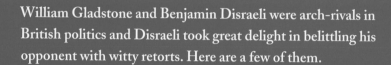

'He has not a single redeeming defect.'

Political brickbats

Gladstone was not a fan of Disraeli's cynical wit, and when the latter claimed he could make fun of any subject, he challenged him to make a joke about Queen Victoria. Disraeli was ready for him, however, and shot back:

'The Queen is not a subject.'

Benjamin Disraeli was once asked to define the difference between a misfortune and a calamity. He replied:

'If Gladstone fell into the Thames, it would be a misfortune. If anybody pulled him out, that, I suppose, would be a calamity.'

Political brickbats

Disraeli didn't come away from the political fray unscathed. Liberal MP John Bright, the man who coined the phrase 'flogging a dead horse', cut him down to size with this appraisal:

'He is a self-made man... and worships his creator.'

Presidential hopeful Bill Clinton brought Vice President Dan Quayle quickly to heel after the latter said he would be 'a pitbull' in the presidential contest. Clinton joked:

'That's got every fire hydrant in America worried.'

Political brickbats

Clement Freud, the British politician, humorist and grandson of the psychoanalyst Sigmund Freud, was a master of the laconic remark. He was the wit who dubbed Margaret Thatcher 'Attila the Hen'. He was once told by a farmer, commenting on inflation:

'Apples are going up.'

To which he replied:

'This would come as a severe blow to Sir Isaac Newton.'

Margaret Thatcher didn't shy away from criticizing others, including those in her own party. No surprise, then, when one of them, Jonathan Aitken, hit back over her lack of knowledge of the Middle East situation with the quip:

'*She probably thinks Sinai is the plural of sinus.*'

British Prime Minister David Cameron replying
to a dig from the opposition:

'I am sure that you
enjoy a game of
bingo; it's the only
time you will ever get
close to Number 10.'

Responding to a critical speech by Conservative MP Geoffrey Howe, Labour MP Denis Healey said:

> '*I must say that part of his speech was rather like being savaged by a dead sheep.*'

Years later, when Howe was appointed Foreign
Secretary, Healey congratulated him in Parliament;
to which Howe replied that it felt like…

*' being nuzzled
by an old ram'.*

When a Latin American diplomat told a lady at a dinner that his country's most popular sport was bullfighting, she replied:

'I've always thought that was revolting.'

The diplomat took this remark in his stride and replied:

'No, that's our second most popular pastime.'

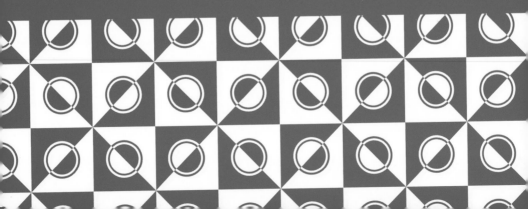

When Reverend Edward Everett Hale, chaplain of the US Senate, was asked if he prayed for the Senators, he deadpanned:

'No, I look at the Senators and pray for the country.'

Back in the day, author Jim Hightower was asked what he thought of his president:

'If ignorance goes to $40 a barrel, I want drilling rights to George Bush's head.'

Political brickbats

Sir Eric Phipps was British ambassador to Germany during the rise of the Nazis in the 1930s. On one occasion, he was kept waiting for a meeting by Hermann Goering, who offered the excuse that he had been at a shooting party. Phipps responded tersely:

`Animals, I hope.´

One of Winston Churchill's closest allies, Frederick Smith, 1st Earl of Birkenhead, better known as F. E. Smith, was every bit as caustic as his friend, even when asked about Churchill himself.

'He devoted the best years of his life to preparing his impromptu speeches,'

he once said of the great orator. Not forgetting,

'*Winston is a man of simple tastes – he is quite easily satisfied with the best of everything.*'

Political brickbats

In response to a complaint from the British
trade unionist Jimmy Thomas that

'I 'ave an 'eadache,'

F. E. Smith replied:

'You need
a couple of
aspirates'

Henry McMaster in a debate with 64-year-old Senator Fritz Hollings:

'You should take a drug test.'

Hollings:

'I'll take a drug test if you'll take an IQ test.'

Political brickbats

Much speculation remains over the incident at the UN General Assembly in 1960, when Soviet leader Nikita Khrushchev took his shoe off and started hitting the table with it in protest at a speech by Filipino delegate Lorenzo Sumulong. A nice little detail was the response of British Prime Minister Harold Macmillan, who allegedly turned to the interpreters and said:

'Could I have that translated, please?'

Congressmen Henry Clay and John Randolph were not the best of friends. Once, when encountering one another on a narrow Washington street, Randolph refused to stand aside, snarling:

'I never sidestep skunks.'

Clay calmly claimed victory by stepping aside and saying:

'I always do.'

Political brickbats

British Prime Minister Harold Wilson claimed to have had a deprived childhood, to which fellow MP Ivor Bulner-Thomas replied:

'If ever he went to school without any boots it was because he was too big for them.'

Responding to news that George W. Bush worked out in order to clear his mind, comedian Jay Leno commented:

'Sometimes a little too much.'

John McCain, when asked what he thought of the idea
of being John Kerry's vice-president, answered:

'I spent several years in a
North Vietnamese POW camp,
kept in the dark,
fed with scraps. Do you
think I want to do that
all over again?'

British Conservative MP William Hague, during a debate with Labour rival John Prescott, listened to his opponent's comments and then, mocking his northern dialect, said:

'There was so little English in that answer, President Chirac would have been happy with it.'

Political brickbats

Prescott got his own back on Hague, now a former Conservative Party leader, when he saw him back on the front bench of the House of Commons:

'The Tories are now so green they're even recycling their leaders.'

Asked for his opinion on Gerald Ford, Lyndon Johnson replied:

'He's a nice guy, but he played too much football with his helmet off.'

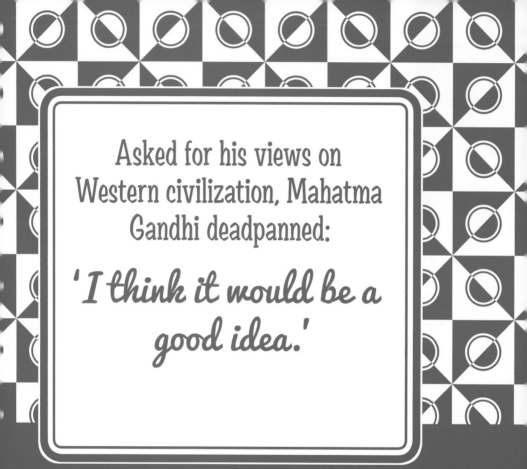

Asked for his views on Western civilization, Mahatma Gandhi deadpanned:

'I think it would be a good idea.'

Former American senator Bob Dole summed up his views on three former leaders of the Free World, Jimmy Carter, Gerald Ford and Richard Nixon, with this brutal assessment:

'History buffs probably noted the reunion at a Washington party a few weeks ago of three ex-presidents, Carter, Ford and Nixon—See No Evil, Hear No Evil, and Evil.'

A Nazi officer in Paris, on discovering Pablo Picasso's masterpiece *Guernica*, which portrays the destruction of the Spanish town by the Luftwaffe during the Spanish Civil War, demanded:

'Did you do that?'

Picasso replied:

'No, you did.'

In a war of words with rival politician John Howard, Australian Prime Minister Paul Keating described his adversary thus:

'He's just a shiver looking for a spine to run up.'

Political brickbats

When Kaiser Wilhelm II tried to intimidate the Dutch Queen Wilhelmina by bragging that his guardsmen were all seven feet tall, she replied:

'But when we open our dykes, the waters are ten feet deep.'

When US president Ronald Reagan was recovering from being shot by a would-be assassin, one of his aides came by to lift his spirits. On being reassured that the government was functioning normally in his absence, Reagan showed that his sense of humour was still intact by replying:

' What makes you think I'd be happy about that?'

US statesman Henry Clay to his bitter rival Thomas Reed:

'I would rather be right than be president.'

Reed's retort:

'The gentleman need not trouble himself. He'll never be either.'

Asked who he voted for, W. C. Fields responded,

'Hell, I never vote for anybody, I always vote against.'

Political brickbats

Winston Churchill wasn't always the darling of British politics. He had regular run-ins with rival politicians, which gave him the chance to wield his famous wit. Churchill's comebacks would almost merit a book on their own, but here's a selection of his wittiest.

MP:

'Mr Churchill, must you fall asleep while I'm speaking?'

Churchill:

'No, it's purely voluntary.'

Churchill was once disturbed on the toilet by word that the Lord Privy Seal was demanding to see him. He barked back:

'*Tell him I can only deal with one sh*t at a time.*'

~~~~~~~~~~~~~~~~~~~~~~~~

Churchill was similarly acerbic when asked about Clement Attlee:

'**A modest man, who has much to be modest about.**'

And when confronted by a woman proclaiming:

'By the year 2100, women will rule the world.'

Churchill replied:

'Still?'

Chapter Three

Disrespectfully yours

When we come up against authority, we have a tendency to go one of two ways. We either tug our forelock, hold our tongue and avoid any trouble… or a little devil takes over and we see the badge or the stripes on the lapel as an open invitation to impishness. When confronted with people who expect reverence, there is nothing funnier than not giving it. This chapter reflects the power struggle between master and servant and that singular form of comeback that we sometimes call bare-faced cheek.

Disrespectfully yours

British politician F. E. Smith was a lawyer by profession and his courtroom comebacks left many a judge reeling. Here are a few examples:

Judge: 'I've listened to you for an hour and I'm none the wiser.'

Smith:

'None the wiser, perhaps, my lord, but certainly better informed.'

Judge: 'Mr Smith, have you ever heard of a saying of Bacon – the great Bacon – that youth and discretion are ill-wedded companions?'

Smith: 'Yes, I have. And have you ever heard of a saying of Bacon – the great Bacon – that a much-talking judge is like an ill-tuned cymbal?'

Judge: 'You are extremely offensive, young man.'

Smith: 'As a matter of fact, we both are; but I am trying to be, and you can't help it.'

Disrespectfully yours

Judge: 'What do you suppose I am on the Bench for, Mr Smith?'

Smith:

'It is not for me, your honour, to attempt to fathom the inscrutable workings of Providence.'

US senator Thomas Hart Benton was asked his opinion of presidential hopeful Stephen A. Douglas:

'Douglas can never be president, Sir. His legs are too short and his coat, like a cow's tail, hangs too near the ground, Sir.'

Disrespectfully yours

During a libel suit against the critic John Ruskin, artist James Whistler was challenged by Ruskin's lawyer as to how long a painting had taken him to complete. He replied that it had taken two days, to which the lawyer mockingly asked:

'The labour of two days? Is that for which you ask two hundred guineas?'

The court erupted in applause when Whistler replied:

'No. I ask it for the knowledge of a lifetime.'

There's something about a condemned man that brings out the cheek in him. Such gallows humour scored a rare point against the notorious Judge Jeffreys during the Bloody Assizes of 1685. Jeffreys poked his cane contemptuously into the chest of a defendant and said:

'There is a rogue at the end of my cane.'

Presumably feeling he had nothing to lose, the condemned man replied:

'At which end, my lord?'

Usually, however, it's those doing the condemning who have the last laugh. Sir Francis Bacon, while serving as Lord Chancellor of England, was once confronted by a man charged with murder. The guilty man pleaded for clemency by pointing out that his name was Hogg and that Hogg and Bacon were related. The judge replied coldly:

'Not until it's hung.'

Even in dire straits, Oscar Wilde retained his sense of humour. His fall from grace saw him frogmarched on to a rain-swept railway platform on the way to Reading Gaol. He told the guards:

`*If this is the way Queen Victoria treats her prisoners, she doesn't deserve to have any.*'

President Kennedy was trying to win the support of a group of businessmen by reassuring them that the economy was strong.

'If I wasn't president I would buy stock myself,' he said. To which one sharp-tongued suit shot back:

'If you weren't president, so would I.'

Flying is a serious business – which is always an invitation for irreverence. Pilots leave reports on the plane's performance for engineers to act upon. As you can imagine, the engineers aren't always as respectful of the pilot's authority as perhaps they should be. Here are some examples:

Pilot report: 'Aircraft handles funny.'

Engineer's report:

'Aircraft warned to straighten up, fly right, and be serious.'

Disrespectfully yours

Pilot report: 'Friction locks cause throttle levers to stick.'

Engineer's report:

'That's what they're there for.'

Pilot report: 'Number 3 engine missing.'

Engineer's report:

'Engine found on right wing after brief search.'

Disrespectfully yours

Hardline US educator Horace Dutton Taft was once confronted by the father of a pupil he had just expelled. The man burst into his office and shouted:

'You think you can run this school any damn way you please, don't you?'

Taft coolly replied:

'Your manner is crude and your language vulgar, but you have somehow got the point.'

The police are another authoritarian body that don't always receive the utmost respect. Would you want to be a traffic cop?

Police officer to motorcyclist: 'Do you know why I pulled you over?'

Motorcyclist: 'Cause I wasn't wearing my seatbelt?'

Police officer to motorist: 'Did you see the speed limit sign?'

Motorist: 'Yes, sir. I just didn't see you sitting behind it.'

Disrespectfully yours

Standing up to the force of the law with a ready wit is a game that goes way back through the centuries. In the 1700s, as the rumble of revolution rolled through France, the much admired opera singer Sophie Arnoud was visited by an officer of the law, asking for the names of certain men she had been 'entertaining'. When she claimed to have forgotten all their names, the officer looked at her suspiciously and said:

'But a woman like you ought to remember things like that.'

To which she replied:

'Of course, lieutenant, but with a man like you, I am not a woman like me.'

When Oscar Levant was conscripted during World War II, he was asked whether he thought he could bring himself to kill. He contemplated the question for a moment and then said:

'I don't know about strangers, but friends, yes.'

For immigration purposes, film director Alfred Hitchcock put his profession down as 'Producer'. When asked by a customs official:

'What do you produce?'

Hitchcock replied:

'Gooseflesh.'

When asked by a US customs official if he was a practising homosexual, the writer Quentin Crisp claims to have replied:

'No need. I'm perfect at it now.'

US customs official to Oscar Wilde:
'Anything to declare?'

Wilde:

'I have nothing to declare but my genius.'

When asked to list his dependants on his tax return, a New York tax payer wrote:

'12.1 million illegal immigrants, 1.1 million crackheads, 4.4 million unemployed deadbeats, 80,000 criminals in over 85 prisons, at least 450 idiots in Congress and numerous others who call themselves politicians but are, in fact, nothing of the sort.'

When the IRS told him his response was unacceptable, he wrote back:

'I thought it was quite detailed. Who did I leave out?'

Disrespectfully yours

The cheek can work both ways, of course.

Chatty barber to 4th century Macedonian prince Archelaus:

'How would you like your hair trimmed, Your Highness?'

Archelaus:

'In silence.'

Chapter Four

Work in progress

When it comes to work, a way with words can be a big advantage. Whether negotiating fees, defending your patch or just responding to enquiries, a light-hearted approach usually wins the day, especially if you can lace your responses with a little laconic wit.

Work in progress

It helps to know your own value. Charles Steinmetz, electrical pioneer, was called in to the General Electric Company to help identify a fault. He examined the equipment and drew a chalk mark on what he believed to be the faulty part. His assessment proved right and he submitted a bill for $10,000. When the accounts department questioned the size of the fee just for making a chalk mark, he sent in the following itemized bill:

'Making chalk mark: $1.00. Knowing where to place it: $9,999.00.'

Lawyer Clarence Darrow was once asked by a grateful client how he could show his appreciation for Darrow's sterling defence of him. Darrow answered eloquently:

'Ever since the Phoenicians invented money, there has only ever been one answer to that question.'

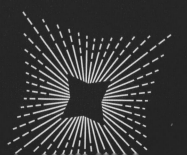

Work in progress

London restaurateur Peter Langan was called over by a diner complaining about a dead cockroach in her food. Langan, echoing the classic 'fly in my soup' gag, replied:

'Madam, it must have come from next door. All our cockroaches are alive.'

While dining in a restaurant, French playwright Georges Feydeau was presented with a lobster that was missing a claw. The waiter explained that it must have lost the claw in a fight with another lobster. Feydau replied:

'Then take this back and bring me the winner!'

Work in progress

American writer Irwin Shaw was at a restaurant in Paris, where the service was painfully slow. Eventually the maître d' approached the table and announced that the house speciality was snails. Shaw replied:

'I know, and you have them dressed as waiters.'

Groucho Marx was once mistaken for the gardener while tending his flower beds.

'How much does the lady of the house pay you?' called a passing lady.

Marx replied:

'The lady of the house? She just lets me sleep with her.'

Work in progress

Journalist to Pope John XXIII:

'How many people work in the Vatican?'

Pope John XXIII:

About half.

~~~~~~~~~~~~~~~~~~~~~~~~~~~~~~~~~~~~

Publisher's telegram to author Graham Greene after receiving his manuscript for *Travels With My Aunt*:

'TERRIFIC BOOK, BUT WE'LL NEED TO CHANGE TITLE.'

Greene's reply:

'NO NEED TO CHANGE TITLE. EASIER TO CHANGE PUBLISHERS.'

Telegram from unknown editor to publisher:

'MUST HAVE RAISE OR COUNT ME OUT.'

Reply from publisher:

'One, two, three, four, five, six, seven, eight, nine, ten.'

Writer and actor Robert Benchley was leaving a hotel when he saw a man in uniform.

'My good man, would you please get me a taxi?' he asked.

The uniformed man replied indignantly: 'I'm not a doorman. I happen to be a rear admiral in the United States Navy.'

Unflinching, Benchley replied:

'All right then, get me a battleship.'

Field Marshal Montgomery, known affectionately as 'Monty' during World War II, hailed a taxi in London and asked the driver to take him to Waterloo. When the driver asked:

'Station?'

Monty replied:

'Well, we're a bit late for the battle.'

Work in progress

An autograph hunter once wrote to Rudyard Kipling, saying:

'I see you get a dollar a word for your writing. I enclose a check for one dollar. Please send me a sample.'

Kipling wrote back:

'Thanks.'

Famous newspaper mogul William Randolph Hearst once sent a bullish telegram to *New York Tribune* owner Whitelaw Reid, asking:

'HOW MUCH WILL YOU TAKE FOR THE TRIBUNE?'

Reid brushed off the takeover bid with this disingenuous reply:

'THREE CENTS ON WEEKDAYS. FIVE CENTS ON SUNDAYS.'

Work in progress

US Secretary of State Dean Acheson described
President Lyndon Johnson as:

'A real centaur: part man, part horse's ass!'

Chapter Five

Slings and arrows

'The pen,' wrote William Shakespeare, 'is mightier than the sword.' And when it comes to conflict, a few well-chosen words can cut much deeper than the sharpest of weapons. This seems to be particularly true in the literary and entertainment world, where the precious, the needy, the superior, the jealous, the exasperated and, of course, the witty prowl around looking for victims upon whom to hone their sharpest lines.

Director George Abbott, when asked by a young method actor what his motivation should be, replied:

'Your job!'

Christopher Plummer described working with actress Julie Andrews as like 'being hit over the head with a Valentine card'. But she belied her image when she unleashed this zinger against journalist Joyce Haber:

'She needs open-heart surgery, and they should go in through her feet.'

Slings and arrows

On one occasion, when the librettist W. S. Gilbert was looking around for an actress he wanted to speak to, he was told by one of the crew:

'She's round behind.'

Gilbert couldn't resist:

'Yes, I know that, but where is she?'

Gilbert was getting annoyed with an actor during a rehearsal one day when the actor lost his temper and hit back:

'I will not be bullied, sir! I know my lines.'

Gilbert retorted:

'Possibly, but you don't know mine.'

Renowned film director Billy Wilder was once having a business meeting with a young studio executive, who had the temerity to ask Wilder to fill him in on what he had done in his career. Wilder simply replied:

'After you.'

Young actor to an ageing Henry Fonda:

'What is the most important thing a young actor has to know?'

Fonda:

'How to become an old actor.'

Slings and arrows

After filming wrapped up on the appropriately titled bill of
Divorcement, Katharine Hepburn turned to her co-star John
Barrymore and said:

'Thank goodness I don't have to act with you anymore.'

Barrymore replied:

'I didn't know you ever had, darling.'

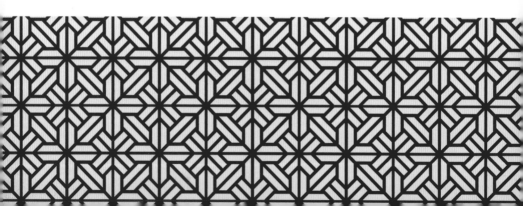

Poor Katharine Hepburn. She once said to Spencer Tracy:

'I'm afraid I'm a little tall for you, Mr Tracy.'

He replied:

'Not to worry, Miss Hepburn, I'll soon cut you down to size.'

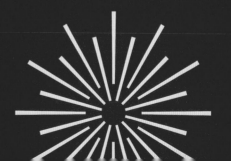

Tracy was challenged by director Garson Kanin on his policy of always making sure his name appeared before his female co-stars on the bill.

'How about ladies first?' suggested Kanin.

Tracy shot back:

'This is a movie, not a lifeboat.'

When hearing how famed method actor Dustin Hoffman had prepared for a harrowing scene in *Marathon Man* by going clubbing, partying, sleeping around and generally wearing himself out, his co-star Laurence Olivier replied:

'Why not try acting?'

Slings and arrows

Ageing actress Alison Skipworth said to the younger Mae West:

'You forget, I've been an actress for 40 years.'

West replied:

'Don't worry, dear. I'll keep your secret.'

Equally vicious was Miriam Hopkins' response to a singer who told her:

'You know, my dear, I insured my voice for $50,000.'

Hopkins replied:

'*That's wonderful. And what did you do with the money?*'

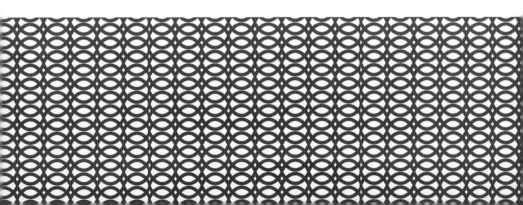

Slings and arrows

Bette Davis and Joan Crawford exchanged many barbs. Davis was the greater wit, both on screen and off, so Crawford was playing a dangerous game when she said:

'Miss Davis was always partial to covering up her face in motion pictures. She called it "Art". Others might call it camouflage – a cover-up for the absence of any real beauty.'

Davis' ripostes always had a touch of humour. For example:

'Joan always cries a lot. Her tear ducts must be close to her bladder.'

Asked once why she was so good at playing bitches, Davis spotted an irresistible opportunity:

'I think it's because I'm not a bitch. Maybe that's why Miss Crawford always plays ladies.'

Writers Gore Vidal and Norman Mailer had an ongoing feud, which involved Mailer physically attacking Vidal on a couple of occasions. After the second attack, when Mailer punched him in the face, Vidal continued his disparagement of the writer, saying:

`Once again, words fail him.´

Vidal and Truman Capote were not the best of friends either. When Vidal was informed of Capote's death, he is alleged to have commented:

'Good career move.'

The Gallagher brothers, Noel and Liam, of Oasis, have spent their career acting out the antithesis of brotherly love, with a tit-for-tat exchange of insults spanning two decades. Liam's digs at Noel usually rely on profanity rather than wit, but Noel clinched the intellectual high ground when he borrowed from Brendan Behan to describe Liam as:

'A man with a fork in a world of soup.'

Composer Thomas Beecham became embroiled in a spat with a woman on a train, who took offence when he complained about her smoking.

'I'll have you know that I am one of the directors' wives,' she told him.

Beecham replied:

'It wouldn't make any difference to me if you were the director's only wife.'

Slings and arrows

What is it with composers? Rossini and Wagner were from very different schools when it came to writing opera, and Rossini – the elder of the two – was quite disparaging about Wagner's 'music of the future', as it was dubbed. Rossini is quoted as having said:

'Wagner has lovely moments but awful quarters of an hour.'

On another occasion Rossini criticized one of Wagner's works thus:

'One cannot judge Lohengrin from a first hearing... and I certainly do not intend to hear it a second time.'

Slings and arrows

But Wagner got his retaliation in with this comeback of comebacks:

'After Rossini dies, who will there be to promote his music?'

It was during a performance of Wagner's *Lohengrin* that Czechoslovakian tenor Leo Slezak brought the house down with a witty ad lib. A technical error meant that the swan boat he was supposed to sail off on at the end of the opera went off without him aboard! Slezak coolly turned to his co-star and asked:

'What time is the next swan?'

Slings and arrows

Actress Lillian Braithwaite received a provocative message from critic James Agate, saying he considered her the 'second most beautiful woman in London'. He clearly wanted her to enquire as to who he thought was the most beautiful, but she refused to take the bait and instead sent back the message:

'Thank you, James. I shall always cherish that, coming from our second-best dramatic critic.'

Satirist Oliver Herford bumped into actor Dustin Farnum and made the mistake of asking how things were going. Farnum answered immodestly: 'I've never been better! My new play is a smash hit. Why, only yesterday, I had the audience glued to their seats.'

Herford replied:

'How clever of you to think of it.'

Slings and arrows

When an audience member threw a rotten cabbage at Oscar Wilde, as he took a bow after a performance of *The Importance Of Being Earnest*, Wilde sniffed the cabbage and said:

'Thank you, my dear fellow. Every time I smell it, I shall be reminded of you.'

After a brief row between Oscar Wilde and Sarah Bernhardt, Wilde asked:

'Do you mind if I smoke?'

Bernhardt snapped back:

'I don't mind if you burn.'

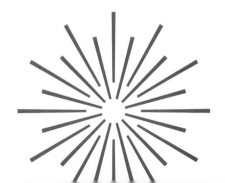

Lily Tomlin was asked for her thoughts on love:

' If love is the answer, can you please rephrase the question?'

~~~~~~~~~~~~~~~~~~~~~~~~~~~~~~~~~

Theatrical agent to critic George S. Kaufman:

'So how do we get our leading lady's name in *The Times*?'

Kaufman:

'Shoot her.'

Actress Jean Harlow allegedly piqued Countess Margot
Asquith by pronouncing the 't' in her name, as in 'harlot'.
Asquith's reply is legendary:

'No, my dear. The t is silent, as in Harlow.'

When George VI and the Duchess of York made their grand entrance to watch a performance of *Tonight at 8:30* starring Noel Coward and Gertrude Lawrence, Lawrence whispered to Coward:

'What an entrance!'

To which Coward responded:

'What a part!'

George Bernard Shaw sent the following caustic invitation to Winston Churchill:

'Am enclosing two tickets to the first night of my new play. Bring a friend. If you have one.'

Churchill replied in kind:

'Cannot possibly attend first night, will attend second. If there is one.'

Slings and arrows

Woody Allen was once asked by a reporter:

'Without naming names, is there anyone in the theatre who has hurt you so much that you want revenge?'"

Allen replied:

'Revenge is putting it mildly. A lady from Queens sitting next to me at Cats woke me before it was over.'

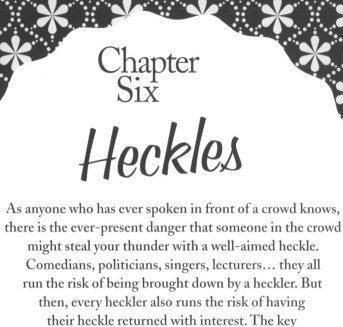

Chapter Six

Heckles

As anyone who has ever spoken in front of a crowd knows, there is the ever-present danger that someone in the crowd might steal your thunder with a well-aimed heckle. Comedians, politicians, singers, lecturers… they all run the risk of being brought down by a heckler. But then, every heckler also runs the risk of having their heckle returned with interest. The key factor is that there is always a crowd there to witness it. Sadly, they are often too drunk to remember it the next morning, but a few have made it on to the record.

Heckles

Eric Douglas, son of *Spartacus* star Kirk Douglas, was doing stand-up in front of a rowdy and disrespectful audience, when he protested:

'You can't do this to me, I'm Kirk Douglas' son!'

A wit in the audience immediately stood up and shouted:

'No, I'm Kirk Douglas' son.'

An audience member in a London comedy club was berated from the stage when he got up to go to the toilet during the act. He came out on top, saying:

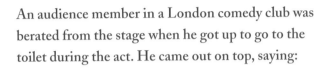

'Sorry, mate, I just wanted to nip to the loo before the comedian starts.'

Heckles

Adlai Stevenson, US ambassador to the UN, was being harangued by a tiresome heckler to make public his beliefs, when he eventually ran out of patience, put down his speech and brought the house down by stating:

'I believe in the forgiveness of sin and the redemption of ignorance.'

A beautiful but possibly apocryphal heckle, perhaps originating from a Robin Williams stand-up gag, concerns a U2 gig in Glasgow. Imagine this really happened. Bono calls for silence and then starts clapping his hands in a slow, regular beat. He speaks into the microphone:

'Every time I clap my hands, a child dies in Africa.'

From the audience comes the cry:

'Stop f***ing doing it then!'

Heckler to English comedian Frank Skinner:

'I met you at medical school.'

Skinner:

'Ah yes, you were the one in the jar.'

George Bernard Shaw gave an eloquent and disarming response to a solitary dissenter after the opening night of *Arms And The Man*. On hearing the man booing while he and the cast took their curtain call, Shaw said:

'I quite agree with you, my friend, but what can we two do against a whole houseful of the opposite opinion?'

Heckles

Harry Hill must be the ultimate unrufflable comedian. His surreal response to a heckler?

'You might heckle me now, but when I get home, I've got a chicken in the oven.'

Steve Martin's response to a heckler:

'Ah, I remember my first beer.'

Poet John Cooper Clarke's response to a heckler:

'*Your bus leaves in ten minutes... Be under it.*'

English comedian Tony Allen, when watching another comedian dying a death on stage, was asked by the unwitting performer what he did for a living.

Allen replied:

'I'm a comedian. What do you do?'

~~~~~~~~~~~~~~~~~~~~~~~~~~~~~

Henry Ward Beecher, US Union campaigner, was once on a tour of the UK when he was asked by a heckler in Manchester why the Union hadn't whipped the Confederates in 60 days, like he had said they would.

Beecher pulled the lion's tail with his reply:

'*Because we found we had Americans to fight this time, not Englishmen.*'

Heckles

One of the most famous sports-related comebacks is of uncertain origin, but let's not worry about that. It is widely credited to the golfer Lee Trevino, who hit a very tricky chip shot over a bunker to within inches of the pin. A man in the crowd called out:

'Are you always that lucky?'

Trevino replied:

'Yep, and the more I practise, the luckier I get.'

US Supreme Court Chief Justice Melville W. Fuller was once faced with a heckler railing against college education. Fuller enquired:

'Do I understand the speaker thanks God for his ignorance?'

When the heckler affirmed, he said:

'Then you have a great deal to be thankful for.'

Heckles

A member of the public once shouted at Australian Prime Minister Robert Gordon Menzies:

'I wouldn't vote for you if you were the Archangel Gabriel!'

Menzies replied:

'If I were the Archangel Gabriel, madam, you would scarcely be in my constituency.'

Philosophy professor Sidney Morgenbesser was attending a lecture on language by British philosopher J. L. Austin. Austin was making the point that two negatives can make a positive but never the other way round, when Morgenbesser pulled the rug from under his feet by drawling a laconic:

'Yeah! Yeah!'

Heckles

US president Teddy Roosevelt had a famous exchange with a heckler that ended with a resounding win for the heckler. Here it is, a warning to all politicians not to follow Roosevelt's line of argument.

Heckler: 'I'm a Democrat.'

Roosevelt: 'May I ask why?'

Heckler: 'My grandfather was a Democrat, my father was a Democrat and I'm a Democrat.'

Roosevelt: 'Suppose your grandfather had been a jackass and your father was a jackass, what would you be then?'

Heckler:

'A Republican!'

Chapter Seven

Cut

Spontaneity is the essence of the witty comeback, but we can't ignore those on-screen ripostes where spontaneous wit trips off the script. Mae West, Groucho Marx, Woody Allen… they're all renowned for their witty one-liners and thankfully for all of us out here, they shared them with us all.

Cut

Let's start with Groucho Marx and an exchange with Chico in *Horse Feathers*:

'There's a man outside with a big black moustache.'

'Tell him I've got one.'

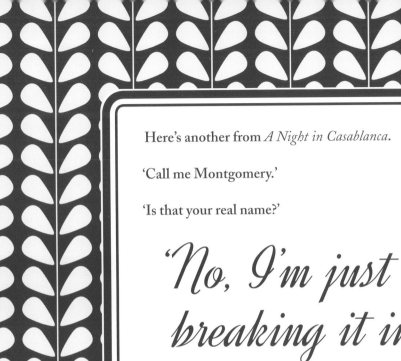

Here's another from *A Night in Casablanca*.

'Call me Montgomery.'

'Is that your real name?'

'No, I'm just breaking it in for a friend.'

Cut

From *A Day at the Races.*
'I've never been so insulted
in my life.'

'Well, it's
early yet.'

Airplane was littered with corny one-liners. Remember this?

'Nervous?'

'Yes.'

'First time?'

'No, I've been nervous lots of times.'

~~~~~~

And this.

'Surely you can't be serious.'

'I am serious... and don't call me Shirley.'

Julia Roberts was gifted a gem of a riposte in *Erin Brockovich*.

'What makes you think you can just walk in there and
take whatever you want?'

'They're called boobs, Ed.'

In *My Fair Lady*, Pickering and Professor Higgins are discussing the latter's plan to use a Covent Garden flower girl for a linguistic experiment.

'Are you a man of good character where women are concerned?'

'Have you ever met a man of good character where women are concerned?'

Cut

James Bond films are peppered with puns. Here are some of the
less corny comebacks.

From *Thunderball*:

'You look pale, Mr Bond, I hope I didn't frighten you.'

'Well, you see, I've always been a nervous passenger.'

'Some men just don't like to be driven.'

'No, some men don't like to be taken for a ride.'

From *The Spy Who Loved Me*:

'Bond! What do you think you're doing?'

'*Keeping the British end up, sir.*'

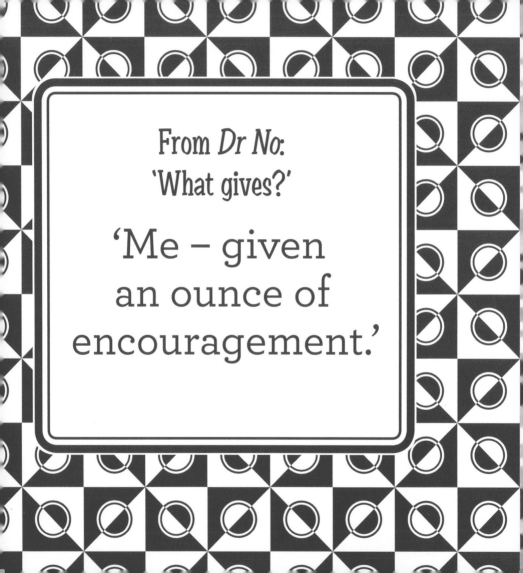

From *Dr No*:
'What gives?'

'Me – given
an ounce of
encouragement.'

From *Octopussy*: 'You suggest a trade. The egg for your life?'

'Well, I heard the price of eggs was going up, but isn't that a little high?'

Cut

Thunderball again:

'That gun… looks more fitting for a woman.'

'Do you know much about guns, Mr Bond?'

'No. I know a little about women.'

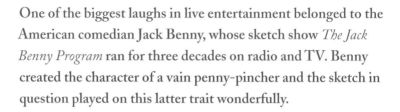

One of the biggest laughs in live entertainment belonged to the American comedian Jack Benny, whose sketch show *The Jack Benny Program* ran for three decades on radio and TV. Benny created the character of a vain penny-pincher and the sketch in question played on this latter trait wonderfully.

Benny is out walking when he is held up by a mugger. The mugger says: 'Your money or your life?' The audience are already laughing as they recognize Benny's dilemma. The mugger, becoming impatient, repeats the challenge:

'Look, bud, I said your money or your life?'

Benny comes back at him sharply:

'I'm thinking it over.'

Cut

In *As Good As It Gets*, irascible novelist Melvin Udall (Jack Nicholson) is asked by a female fan how he manages to write women so well. He leaves her stunned with his outrageous reply:

'I think of a man and then take away reason and accountability.'

Mae West was the mistress of the saucy retort. Some were spontaneous, some scripted. In her Broadway hit *Diamond Lil*, she gave the world this legendary comeback. 'Goodness! What beautiful diamonds.'

'Goodness had nothing to do with it, dearie.'

Cut

In *My Little Chickadee*, West plays the feisty Flower Belle Lee. In one scene she incurs the wrath of the judge for showing a lack of respect in court.

'Are you showing contempt for this court?'

'I'm doing my best to hide it.'

Marilyn Monroe played comedy brilliantly, especially in *Some Like It Hot*, in which she was cast as the smouldering singer Sugar Kane Kowalczyk, hoping to find a millionaire to marry.

'Going to catch yourself a rich bird, eh?'

'Oh, I don't care how rich he is, as long as he has a yacht and his own private railroad car and his own toothpaste.'

In *Gentlemen Prefer Blondes*, she wins the day in this exchange with her prospective father-in-law, Mr Esmond Sr, played by Taylor Holmes, who is suspicious of her motives.

'Have you got the nerve to tell me you aren't marrying him for his money?'

'It's true.'

'Then why do you want to marry him?'

'I want to marry him for your money.'

Marilyn could be on the receiving end too, like this exchange with Jane Russell in the same film.

'You must think I was born yesterday.'

'Well, sometimes there's just no other possible explanation.'

Or this is how a French guard taunts King Arthur in *Monty Python and the Holy Grail*:

'Your mother was a hamster and your father smelt of elderberries!'

Chief Martin Brody's famous response after his first sighting of the shark in *Jaws*:

'We're gonna need a bigger boat.'

Cut

Here's a favourite example of Woody Allen's comic take on life from *Play It Again Sam*. Allen plays Allan, who falls for a rather intense girl (played by Diane Davila) in a museum and tries to ask her out.

'What are you doing Saturday night?'

'Committing suicide.'

'What about Friday night?'

Another Allen classic was this dialogue with Peter O'Toole in a Parisian café in *What's New Pussycat?*

'Did you find a job?'

'Yeah, I got something at the striptease. I help the girls dress and undress.'

'Nice job.'

'Twenty francs a week.'

'Not very much.'

'It's all I can afford.'

And then there's the classic Allen gag from *Annie Hall*.

'What's the difference? It's all mental masturbation.'

'Oh, well, now we're finally getting to a subject you know something about!'

'Hey, don't knock masturbation! It's sex with someone I love.'

Chapter Eight

Cruel to be kind

Honesty, they say, is the best policy. But sometimes the challenge is finding the words to say what you really think without sounding like you really think it. This is where a razor-sharp wit can help you cut the conversation short without looking like a spoilsport. Pay close attention. You never know when you might need one of these.

Benjamin Disraeli was once sent a manuscript from an unknown author, asking for his appraisal. The reluctant Disraeli's response has passed into folklore:

'Thank you for the manuscript. I shall lose no time in reading it.'

Here's another classic play on words, widely attributed to Dorothy Parker but evidently originated by Sid Ziff, a reviewer for the *Los Angeles Mirror-News*:

'This is not a book to be tossed aside lightly. It should be thrown with great force!'

Cruel to be kind

It's the sort of thing Dorothy Parker would have said. She could fill a chapter on her own with her famous witticisms. A priggish young man once made the mistake of putting his head in the lion's mouth when he confided to her:

'I simply cannot bear fools.'

She bit:

'How odd, your mother could.'

In more playful mood, challenged to come up with a witty sentence containing the word 'horticulture', Parker struck gold with:

'You may lead a whore to culture, but you can't make her think.'

But when a friend approached her for advice on what to do
with his old, sick cat, Parker advised:

'*Try curiosity.*'

French satirist Antoine de Rivarol was asked to give his feedback on a two-line poem. He read the lines and said:

'Very nice, although there are dull stretches.'

Cruel to be kind

US President Calvin Coolidge was once enduring a music recital when the person sitting next to him whispered:

'Mr Coolidge, what do you think of the singer's execution?'

Coolidge replied:

'I'm all for it.'

President Calvin Coolidge was renowned for his pithiness. When approached by a lady at a dinner, saying she had had a bet that she could get more than two words out of him, he shot back:

'You lose.'

American writer Carl Sandburg was asked by a young playwright to attend a rehearsal of a new play he had written and give his appraisal. The playwright was annoyed to learn that Sandburg had fallen asleep during the rehearsal and demanded:

'How could you fall asleep when you knew I wanted your opinion?'

Sandburg drawled:

'*Young man, sleep is an opinion.*'

The controversial author Elinor Glyn sent one of her early manuscripts to a London publisher with a note requesting a swift decision as she had 'other irons in the fire'.

The publisher sent the manuscript back with a note:

'Put this with your other irons.'

Cruel to be kind

When asked to offer his appraisal of Jean-Baptiste Rousseau's poem 'Ode to Posterity', French writer Voltaire replied:

'*I do not think this poem will reach its destination.*'

Albert Einstein played a bit of violin and on one occasion he duetted with famous cellist Gregor Piatigorsky.

'Did I play well?' He asked the virtuoso. Piatigorsky replied cheekily:

' You played relatively well.'

Cruel to be kind

Receiving unsolicited criticism is also an art. German composer Max Reger is reponsible for one of the most famous responses to a bad review when he wrote to the critic Rudolph Louis:

' I am sitting in the smallest room in my house. I have your review before me. In a moment it will be behind me.'

Literary wit James Thurber was once told by a friend that he had read the French edition of his book *My Life and Hard Times* and it was even better in French.

Thurber replied:

'Yes, my work tends to lose something in the original.'

Cruel to be kind

The painter Raphael received an unwelcome visit from a group of cardinals, who proceeded to criticize his work. Peering at Raphael's depiction of St Paul, one commented:

'The face of the apostle Paul is far too red.'

Undaunted, Raphael explained:

'He blushes to see into whose hands the church has fallen.'

Cruel to be kind

Sometimes, though, it's good news. Victor Hugo sent the following telegram to his publisher, inquiring about sales of his latest work, *Les Misérables*:

'?'

The publisher replied:

Oscar Wilde gave such free rein to his sardonic wit that it was even, on occasion, turned on his friends. For example, the poet Lewis Morris, who had aspirations to be poet laureate. When his credentials appeared to be ignored, Morris claimed that there was 'a conspiracy of silence' and asked his friend Wilde what he should do. Wilde offered the somewhat heartless rejoinder:

' *Join it.* '

Cuttingly witty artist James McNeill Whistler liked to take on Oscar Wilde in verbal jousts. Once Wilde actually complimented one of Whistler's comments by saying:

'I wish I had said that.'

Whistler pressed home his advantage with the retort:

'You will, Oscar, you will.'

Cruel to be kind

Whistler found himself on the receiving end when Mark Twain called in and started perusing his latest paintings:

'For the love of God!' said Whistler. 'Be careful! The paint is still fresh.'

Twain replied sweetly:

'No need to be concerned.
I have my gloves on.'

The English actress Mrs Patrick Campbell had a mischievous sense of humour. On one occasion she was being bored senseless by a scientist banging on about ants. At one point he pronounced:

'Ants even have their own police force and their own army.'

Mrs Pat deadpanned:

'No navy, I suppose?'

Cruel to be kind

When English writer Oliver Herford was accosted by a fellow club member complaining, 'I just heard somebody in the lobby say he'd offer me fifty dollars to resign my membership. What should I do?' Herford advised his tedious acquaintance:

'Hold out for a hundred.'

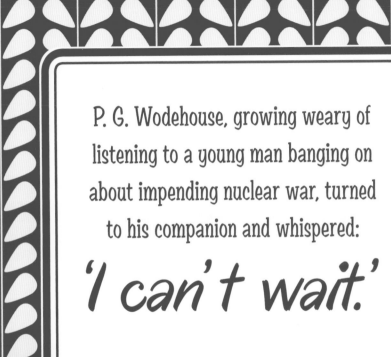

P. G. Wodehouse, growing weary of listening to a young man banging on about impending nuclear war, turned to his companion and whispered:

'I can't wait.'

Cruel to be kind

In arty circles, there's always someone at the party who claims to be writing a book. These great works seldom materialize. English comedian Peter Cook brought this into the light beautifully on one such occasion, when he heard the familiar:

'Did I tell you, Peter? I'm writing a book.'

'No,' he replied. 'Neither am I.'

Chapter Nine

Modesty permits

Not all comebacks are at the expense of the provocateur. Self-effacement can be every bit as witty – and considerably more classy – than conflict. Alas, examples of this art are much rarer than the more offensive kind, so treasure these gems and emulate them when you can.

Modesty permits

Abraham Lincoln was a master at drawing the enemy's sting. When US Senator Stephen Douglas accused him of being two-faced, Lincoln replied:

'I leave it to my audience. If I had another face, do you think I would wear this one?'

And when a foreign diplomat expressed great surprise at seeing him blacking his own boots, Lincoln replied coolly:

'Whose boots do you black?'

Modesty permits

Bob Dole, after losing the Republican nomination to George H. W. Bush, was asked how he had taken the defeat:

'Contrary to reports that I took the loss badly, I slept like a baby. Every two hours I woke up and cried.'

Reporter to William F. Buckley Jr., unfancied candidate to become mayor of New York City:

'What's the first thing you will do if you are elected mayor?'

Buckley:

'Demand a recount.'

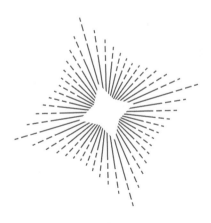

President Kennedy was once asked by a young boy what he had done to become a war hero (he saw service in the US Navy and was decorated for helping his men to rescue after their torpedo boat collided with a Japanese destroyer). Kennedy replied:

'It was involuntary. They sank my boat.'

Later, as US President, he was told that the Republican Nationalist Committee had adopted a resolution saying that he was pretty much a failure. Unfazed, he simply replied:

'I assume it passed unanimously.'

Modesty permits

Clement Freud retained his saucy sense of humour into his 80s, though not the mobility in his knees. He told a story about being asked by a lady to 'come upstairs and make love', to which he replied:

'I'm afraid it has to be one or the other'.

When Steven Spielberg asked John Williams to score the soundtrack for *Schindler's List*, Williams modestly told him:

'You need a better composer than I am to score this film.'

Spielberg replied in kind:

'Yes, I know, but they're all dead.'

The Los Angeles Country Club was a bastion of snobbery and bigotry, with a membership policy that stated 'no Jews, no Catholics and no actors'. But one actor, the Western star Randolph Scott, got around the restriction by writing in his membership application:

'If you've seen any of my pictures, you'll realize I'm no actor.'

It was when asked whether he would be interested in membership of the Los Angeles Country Club that Groucho Marx uttered his immortal retort:

'Why would I want to join a club that would have me as a member?'

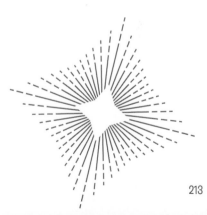

Modesty permits

Asked whether he had any plans for working on the big screen in future, Liberace replied,

'I've done my bit for motion pictures; I've stopped making them.'

Meanwhile Bette Davis and Joan Crawford kept up their verbal feud for decades. Crawford played down any responsibilty:

'Bette likes to rant and rave. I just sit and knit. She yelled and I knitted a scarf from Hollywood to Malibu.'

Modesty permits

When questioned about his views on America looking back after his presidency, Jimmy Carter said:

'*My esteem in this country has gone up substantially. It is very nice that when people wave at me now, they use all their fingers.*'

Chapter Ten

Mob rule OK

We shouldn't confine this compendium of comebacks to
the wit of the rich and famous. After all, there are people
out there being funny every day and happily we have
the evidence, even if we don't always have the name
of the originator. From the subway to the office
to the classroom to the sports stadium, we
have gathered examples of witty comebacks
that prove that ordinary people are all just
entertainers at heart.

Mob rule OK

The sign on the printer said:

'This printer is only here temporarily.'

To which, one office wit responded by note:

' In the greater scheme of things, we all are...'

Exam questions, rather like press interviews, require a quick and intelligent response. Alas, sometimes that intelligence is channelled in the wrong direction. Or the right one, if laughter is more important to you than qualifications.

Q: 'Mary and Mark want to find out the favourite colour among all 300 students in their year. Mary asks 30 people. Mark asks 150. Mark thinks his answer is more likely to be right. Why would he think this?'

A: 'Because he's a man.'

Q: 'Name six animals that live exclusively in the Arctic.'

A: *'Two polar bears. Four seals.'*

Q: 'When Mary looks through her microscope she can't see anything. Suggest one reason why not.'

A: ' She's blind.'

Q: 'Bob has 36 candy bars. He eats 29. What does he have now?'

A: 'Diabetes.'

Q: 'Expand (x-n)2'

A:

$$(x - n) 2$$
$$(x - n) 2$$

Mob rule OK

Q: 'Please explain what hard water is.'

A: 'Ice.'

~~~~~~

Q: 'What ended in 1896?'

A: '1895.'

Q: 'Where was the Declaration of Independence signed?'

A: 'At the bottom.'

Mob rule OK

Q: 'In what state does the Sacramento River flow?'

A: 'Liquid.'

Q: 'What is the strongest force on Earth?'

A: 'Love.'

Mob rule OK

Q: 'Find x.'

A: 'Here it is.'

Billboard campaign ad from US department of health:

'This year thousands of men will die from stubbornness.'

Sprayed riposte:

'No, we won't.'

Mob rule OK

Graffiti on subway wall:

'Question everything.'

Scrawl underneath:

Notice on wall:

'Bill Stickers will be prosecuted.'

Graffiti:

'Bill Stickers is innocent.'

Notice on vending machine:

'Not accepting change.'

Riposte:

'Change is inevitable. Deal with it!'

Notice on another vending machine:

'Warning: This machine takes your money and gives nothing in return.'

Riposte:

'*Just like my ex.*'

Notice on coffee machine:

'Not hot.'

Riposte:

'But has a
great personality.'

Notice on door:

'This door is alarmed.'

Riposte:

'What startled it?'

Mob rule OK

Notice on door of food outlet:

'Closed due to short staff.'

Riposte:

'Please hire taller staff.'

Notice on dorm wall:

'To whoever the idiot is who keeps smoking pot and storing it in the vents, please take it out. I don't want my room smelling of your bad decision.'

Riposte:

'You seem stressed. :)'

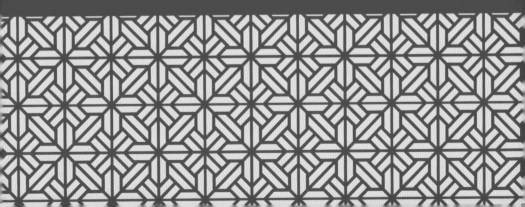

Mob rule OK

Saccharin message on poster:

'Maybe it's not always about trying to fix something that's broken. Maybe it's about starting over and trying to create something better.'

Riposte:

'And that's why you have a younger brother.'

Chapter Eleven

On the spot

If ever you need to be able to think on your feet, it's when being interviewed. After all, the interviewer has had time to prepare the questions; you have to come up with an instant answer. And that's when, if you're lucky, the wit kicks in. Politicians, sports stars, actors and actresses have all had to think up quick answers to sharp questions from the press. And even when the questions aren't so sharp, it's an opportunity to have a bit of fun.

On the spot

Interviewer to baseball player Alex Johnson:

'Alex, you hit only two homers all of last year and this season you already have seven. What's the difference?'

Johnson:

'Five.'

Baseball legend Babe Ruth was one of the game's star sluggers. When challenged during the Great Depression that he had a higher salary than President Hoover, he hit back:

'Maybe so, but I had a better year than he did.'

On the spot

Liverpool FC soccer coach Bill Shankly was a master of the one-liner. Once, in response to an assertion that his defender Roy Evans was not quick enough, he said:

'I agree the lad's pace can be deceptive... he's much slower than you think.'

Shankly's most famous comeback was in response to a question about how seriously he took the game.

'Some people believe football is a matter of life and death... I can assure you it's much more important than that.'

Brian Clough was one of England's most talented soccer managers but also one of its most controversial, largely due to his unshakeable self-belief. The net result was that he gave great quote. Looking back on his career, he was asked how he rated himself as a manager and replied:

'I wouldn't say I was the best in the business, but I was in the top one.'

In reply to a question about the length of time it was taking for a team to take shape, he replied:

'Rome wasn't built in a day. But I wasn't on that particular job.'

On the spot

Asked how he deals with players who question his decisions, he explained:

'Well, I ask him which way he thinks it should be done. We get down to it and then we talk about it for twenty minutes and then we decide I was right.'

When asked about the appointment of Swede Sven-Goran Eriksson as England coach, Clough replied:

'At last England have appointed a manager who speaks English better than the players.'

Asked what he thought of the trend for the long-ball game (huge kicks upfield), he said:

'*If God had wanted us to play football in the clouds, he'd have put grass up there.*'

But the one that made even Clough himself crack a smile came during the 1986 World Cup, when he was working as a TV pundit with ex-England player Mick Channon. When asked by the host about England's apparent inability to play a certain way, Channon began to rant:

'The Irish have done it. The French do it. The West Germans do it. We don't.'

Clough considered his reply for a moment, before offering with a smirk:

'Even educated bees do it.'

On the spot

The actor Cary Grant once intercepted a telegram from a paper to his agent, enquiring:

'HOW OLD CARY GRANT?'

Grant sent the following reply:

'OLD CARY GRANT FINE. HOW YOU?'

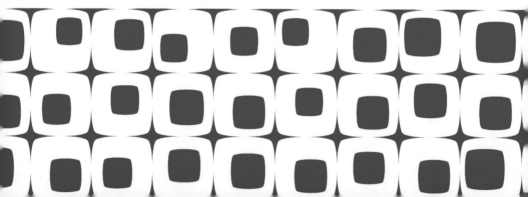

Asked by an interviewer what he thought of New Zealand, British politician and humorist Clement Freud replied:

'I find it hard to say, because when I was there it seemed to be shut.'

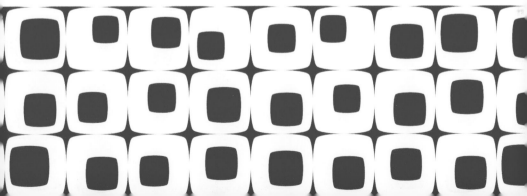

On the spot

When Dolly Parton was asked if she resented being dismissed as a dumb blonde, she showed the description to be false in the best possible manner:

'In the first place, I know I'm not dumb. And I sure as hell know I'm not blond!'

Interviewer to Dolly Parton: 'How long does it take to have your hair done?'

Dolly:

'I don't know. I'm not there when my hair is done.'

On the spot

New York Mayor Ed Koch to persistent reporter
Andrew Kirtzman:

'I can explain this to you; I can't comprehend it for you.'

Reporter to Elvis Presley: 'What's your idea of the ideal girl?'

Elvis replied succinctly:

'Female, sir.'

Interviewer to Mel Brooks: 'You've been accused of vulgarity.'

Brooks:

'Bullsh*t!'

The long-running British radio show *Desert Island Discs* always asks its guests what one book they would want to have with them if they were stranded on a desert island. G. K. Chesterton had his answer ready:

'*Thomas's Guide to Practical Shipbuilding.*'

On the spot

Writer Isaac Bashevis Singer, a vegetarian, was once asked by a reporter whether his vegetarianism was for religious reasons or out of consideration for his health.

Singer replied:

'I do it out of consideration for the chicken'.

Journalist to J. M. Barrie, creator of *Peter Pan*:

'Sir James, I suppose some of your plays do better than others. They're not all successes, are they?'

Barrie (surely not off the cuff):

'No, some peter out and some pan out.'

On the spot

An intrusive reporter came doorstepping Barrie and
when Barrie came to the door said:

'Sir James Barrie, I presume?'

Barrie shot back:

'*You do!*'

James McNeill Whistler was once asked by an incredulous interviewer how come he was born in such an unfashionable place as Lowell, Massachusetts. Whistler replied:

'I wished to be near my mother.'

On the spot

Travel writer John Gunther specialized in books about Europe, South America, etc. Late in his life he was asked:

'What will you do when you run out of continents?'

Gunther deadpanned:

'Try incontinence.'

The Beatles were well-known for their witty interviews.
In fact, few reporters got a straight answer from any of them.
For example:

Reporter to George Harrison:

'Where do the hair-dos come from?'

John Lennon interjecting:

'The scalp.'

263

On the spot

Reporter to The Beatles:

'How did you find America?'

John Lennon:

'Turned left at Greenland.'

In 1959, Liberace sued the UK's *Daily Mirror* over an article that alleged he was gay. He sent the paper a note, saying:

'What you said hurt me very much. I cried all the way to the bank.'

Asked for her views on sexual equality, Marilyn Monroe quipped:

'Women who seek to be equal with men lack ambition.'

When a false story arose that Mark Twain had died while on a visit to England, Twain sent a telegram to the *New York Journal* stating:

'THE REPORT OF MY DEATH WAS AN EXAGGERATION.'

On the spot

Poet Maxwell Bodenheim once took part in a debate with playwright Ben Hecht, who proposed the motion 'That people who attend literary debates are imbeciles'. After Hecht had delivered his speech in favour of the motion, Bodenheim stood up, surveyed the audience, turned to his opponent and said:

'You win.'

Soviet President Mikhail Gorbachev was once asked what might have happened if Khrushchev had been assassinated instead of JFK. Gorbachev deadpanned:

'I don't think Mr Onassis would have married Mrs Khrushchev.'

Reporter to Noel Coward on a miserable day in London:

'Mr Coward, have you anything to say to the *Sun*?'

Coward:

'Shine.'

During the McCarthy era of communist witchhunts in the US, Robert Hutchins, president of the University of Chicago, was once challenged by a right-wing journalist, who asked:

'Is communism still being taught at the university?'

Hutchins dismissed the accusation with:

'Yes, and cancer at the medical school.'

On the spot

Ronald Reagan was America's oldest President and when, during his re-election contest with Walter Mondale, he was questioned by a reporter as to whether his age might be a hindrance to running the country in a crisis, he replied that he was 'not going to make age an issue of this campaign' and added:

'I am not going to exploit for political purposes my opponent's youth and inexperience.'

When questioned on the subject of abortion, Reagan quipped:

'I've noticed that everyone who is for abortion has already been born.'

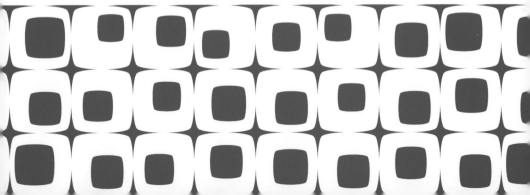

On the spot

Helen Reddy started her career as an entertainer at the age of four and made easy listening records. During the 1970s, she enjoyed hit after hit including her signature song, 'I Am Woman'. But when rival Bette Midler was asked what she thought of Reddy's singing, she memorably said:

'She ought to be arrested for loitering in front of an orchestra.'

Reporter to the prolific actor Spencer Tracy:

'What do you look for in a script?'

Tracy:

'Days off.'

On the spot

When asked about celebrity and being recognized in public, the renowned physicist Stephen Hawking explained:

'The wheelchair gives me away.'

When T.S. Eliot was asked if he agreed with the
contention that most editors are failed writers, he replied:

'Perhaps, but so are most writers.'

Baseball coach Yogi Berra was legendary for his amusing statements and comments, which cropped up frequently in his press conferences – although he once claimed: 'I never said all the things I said.' On one occasion he told the gathered media:

'If you ask me anything I don't know, I'm not going to answer.'

Chapter Twelve

Naughty but nice

This section is for readers who like things that are naughty but nice. Still reading? Of course you are! This chapter covers various vices. After all, some of the most impactful comebacks involve a little shock. So this is where the responses get spicy and we tickle your fancy with fruity references to things that pique the proclivities of polite company and elicit a gasp, followed by a giggle.

Naughty but nice

Mae West was never lost for words on the subject of love.

'When choosing between two evils, I always like to try the one I've never done before.'

Chico Marx was once accused by his wife Betty of kissing another girl at a party. He pleaded:

'I wasn't kissing her, I was whispering in her mouth.'

Naughty but nice

Groucho Marx, hosting a TV gameshow, was told by a woman contestant that the reason she had 11 children was because she loved her husband. Marx brought the nation to a standstill with his reply:

'Well, I love my cigar but I take it out of my mouth once in a while.'

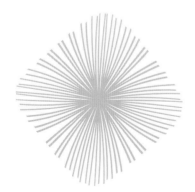

Dorothy Parker often used her wit to shock:

'If all the young ladies who attended the Yale prom were laid end to end, no one would be the least surprised.'

Naughty but nice

A naughty riposte, which has been variously attributed to Groucho Marx, Winston Churchill, Mark Twain, Lord Beaverbrook and others, and varies in the exact wording, goes roughly like this. A man and a lady are playing a game of hypothetical questions.

Man: 'Would you sleep with me for ten thousand dollars?'

Lady: 'You know, I think I just might.'

Man: 'What if I offered you five dollars?'

Lady: 'Certainly not! What kind of woman do you think I am?'

Man:

'We've already established that. Now we're just haggling over the price.'

Female speaker campaigning for the temperance movement:

'I would rather commit adultery than take a glass of beer.'

Male voice from the crowd:

'Who wouldn't?'

Naughty but nice

Sign outside church:

'If tired of sin, come in.'

Graffiti written underneath:

'If not, call 555-4321.'

Woman to Irish lawyer Lord Charles Russell:

'What is the maximum punishment for bigamy?'

Russell:

'Two mothers-in-law.'

Actor George Raft is credited with originating a retort that has since been attributed to other notorious hedonists, such as soccer player George Best and W. C. Fields. When asked what had happened to all his earnings, Raft explained:

'Part of the loot went for gambling, part for horses, and part for women. The rest I squandered.'

When President John Adams was challenged over a rumour that he had sent one of his generals to Europe to bring back four mistresses to share between the two of them, Adams dispelled the scandal by answering,

'*I do declare, if this be true, General Pinckney has kept them all for himself, and cheated me out of my two.*'

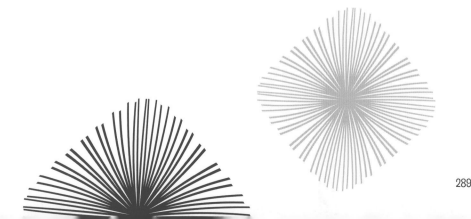

Naughty but nice

Mae West was never short of advice on the subject of sex:

'Cultivate your curves - they may be dangerous but they won't be avoided.'

British lawyer and politician John Horne Tooke replied to suggestions that he should 'take a wife' with the risqué retort:

'With all my heart, whose wife shall it be?'

Naughty but nice

The Irish scholar John Pentland Mahaffy is credited with this intellectually witty piece of wordplay.

Woman: 'What's the difference between a man and a woman?'

Man:

'Madam, I cannot conceive.'

During the Profumo Affair trial in London in the 1960s, the defence counsel challenged showgirl Mandy Rice-Davies with the question:

'Are you aware that Lord Astor denies any impropriety in his acquaintanceship with you?'

Rice-Davies caused uproar in the courtroom with her cheeky reply:

' Well, he would, wouldn't he?'

Naughty but nice

When a friend of playwright Marc Connelly stroked his bald head and told him it felt like his wife's backside, Connelly felt his own head and said:

'So it does, so it does.'

An amusing story exists, which may or may not be true, about Noah Webster, who compiled the *American Dictionary of the English Language*. As the story goes, Webster was caught by his wife in flagrante with his chambermaid.

'Noah!' she exclaimed. 'I'm surprised!'

Webster, unable to resist his compulsion for the correct use of vocabulary, looked up from his compromising position and replied:

'No, my dear, I am surprised. You are astonished.'

Journalist to Peggy Guggenheim:

'How many husbands have you had?'

Guggenheim:

'Do you mean my own or other people's?'

Asked if he 'did' drugs, surrealist painter Salvador Dali replied:

*'I don't do drugs.
I am drugs.'*

Naughty but nice

Truman Capote was once confronted by a man who was jealous that his wife was asking Capote for his autograph. The man pulled out his penis and suggested Capote autographed that, to which the writer coolly responded:

'I don't know if I can autograph it but perhaps I can initial it.'

When asked if he agreed with the notion of clubs for women, W. C. Fields replied impishly:

'Certainly, but only if all other means of persuasion fail.'

Naughty but nice

Socialist Clement Attlee was a regular victim of Winston Churchill's caustic humour. On one occasion he found himself in the company of his adversary at a urinal, albeit with Winston standing as far away as he could.

'Feeling standoffish today, are we, Winston?' said Attlee, to which Churchill replied:

'That's right. Every time you see something big, you want to nationalize it.'

Chapter Thirteen

The last laugh

It is one of the human race's saving graces that the thought of death stokes our sense of humour. A witty one-liner on a headstone has to be the ultimate comeback – a refusal to be cowed by the call of the Grim Reaper. So before we move on to famous last words and deathbed denials, let's begin with some amusing epitaphs spotted in graveyards around the world.

'I came here without being consulted and I leave without my consent.'

'I knew
this would
happen.'

The last laugh

Humphrey Bogart's headstone reads:

'I should never have switched from Scotch to Martinis.'

Mel Blanc, aka the Man of 1,000 Voices, was the voice of numerous Warner Brothers' cartoon characters, including Bugs Bunny, Daffy Duck, Road Runner, Yosemite Sam and Percy Pig. On his headstone are the immortal words:

'*That's all, folks.*'

American talk show host Merv Griffin's headstone reads:

'I will not be right back after this message.'

Peter Ustinov:

'Please keep off the grass.'

The last laugh

Rodney Dangerfield:

'There goes the neighborhood.'

Comedian Spike Milligan's headstone bears the Irish inscription '*Duirt me leat go raibh me breoite.*' It means:

'I told you I was ill.'

The elderly US Senator Chauncey Depew was once asked what he thought of taking regular exercise, to which he replied:

'I get my exercise by acting as a pallbearer to my friends who exercise.'

When the showman Eubie Blake was celebrating his 100th birthday, he was asked how he felt. He replied:

' If I'd known I was going to live this long, I'd have taken better care of myself!'

The last laugh

Friend to George S. Kaufman during an intellectual
discussion about suicide:

'So, how would you kill yourself?'

Kaufman:

'With kindness.'

Priest to Henry David Thoreau:

'Have you made your peace with God?'

Thoreau:

'I was not aware we had ever quarrelled.'

The last laugh

Physician to Pausanius, the Spartan general:

'You have lived to be an old man.'

Pausanius:

'That is because I never employed you as my physician.'

On his deathbed, Voltaire was beseeched by a priest to renounce the Devil, to which he asked:

'Is this a time to be making enemies?'

The last laugh

On his deathbed, W. C. Fields, a renowned atheist, was found flicking through the Bible. Asked what he was doing, he replied:

'Looking for loopholes.'

W. S. Gilbert was once discreetly trying to convey to an unwitting friend that a famous composer had died. When the man asked if he was still composing, Gilbert replied somewhat indelicately (you can see it coming):

'*On the contrary, he is decomposing.*'

The very last laugh is courtesy of Father Andrew Agnellus, religious adviser to the BBC, who was once asked by a producer how he could find out the official Catholic view of Heaven and Hell. Agnellus' reply was short and sweet:

'Die.'